Embracing *the* Storm Within

Embracing the Storm Within

Poems of Vulnerability, Love and Joy

Debarati Chakraborty

EXCELLER BOOKS®
A GLOBAL PRESS

Embracing the Storm Within
Poems of Vulnerability and Joy

Cover by Exceller Books using resources from Pixabay.com

ISBN: 978-93-48892-33-1

Published in India in 2025 by Exceller Books,
An imprint of GE Group,
G1, Dream Apartment, Degree College Road, Belgharia,
Kolkata, 700056, India
www.excellerbooks.com

EXCELLER BOOKS®
A GLOBAL PRESS

Dedication

Baba Ma, and Chunu (my saviour, my whole heart, my cat, forever in my heart)

Acknowledgment

I was never told, "You cannot do this." And for this, my biggest cheerleaders have been my parents, a few of my teachers, and two friends (Utsha and Sahana) who always believed in me, even when I had lost hope in myself. I believe the more you are grateful, the more the universe gives you occasions to be grateful for. I started scribbling from a very tender age. During those times, I took inspiration mostly from the beautiful nature I was surrounded by. My home away from home, Oak Grove School, Mussoorie.

Whatever I am today is only because of how my school shaped me, and I can never deny that fact. I think boarding schools teach you a lot of life's lessons and values unknowingly. That being said, I hope you love reading the poems as much as I loved weaving them into this book.

Contents

A Memoir of Childhood

The Calcutta Memoir

Freedom

Cocoon

Taunted, suppressed, scolded upon,
Lived a girl in her cocoon.
The times she tried to lift herself free,
She was silenced to breathe.
She breathed every breath, but something
Kept hindering her.
She kept living in her cocoon until
One day she saw her reflection in the mirror.
A butterfly, as beautiful as it may seem,
Was seen flying free in the image.
She questioned her belonging,
She questioned her might.
She tried to break free,
But she was still consumed in thoughts of fear—
Fear of this world,
Fear of all the unseen things in front.
She kept watching her arms pull out,
She kept watching herself pull out.
She was out of her cocoon,
Still afraid of the unknown.
But she spread her arms as if they were wings
And tried to fly.
She failed at every possible flight;
She was again pushed back by her very own.
She tried again in silence and dark,
And one day she broke away from the catastrophe.
She flew towards the light,
Enjoying life's nectar, just like a butterfly.
Her fears vanished as she no longer waited for validation.

She was free from all the pain, worries, and fears;
She was free from her small world.
She blossomed,
She bloomed,
She conquered whatever she could.
She is us,
She is you—
Break through, for the world might be waiting for you.

Mirror

Mirroring the mother
I dressed up as beautiful as her.
The image in front gave all the validation
I needed to look like a woman.
Kept looking at myself for hours,
Felt like a woman in all my powers.
I was shunned every time I dressed up like my mum,
Not knowing what was wrong with the form.
My inner self always screamed of grace,
But I was born to be a male.
My body looked otherwise
Than the person I was from inside.
All I ever wanted was to look like my mother.
I was bullied,
I was pushed away,
I was muted—
For who I wanted to be,
For who I am from inside.
But my outer body looked otherwise.
Amidst all the screams in my head,
I dressed myself again.
The mockery from around
Didn't bother me ever again.
I felt like a woman,
I looked like a woman,
And there is no shame
I feel to live this moment.

I am her.
I am the divine,
I am everything that my heart desires.

Colours of Love

As I sit by my window,
I see a boy staring at me from afar.
Every now and then, his gaze meets mine.
Years passed by,
And I returned home again.
I sat on that same old chair
And opened the window,
Hoping to see his bright face.
All these years away,
There was not a single day
His thoughts didn't cross my mind.
I often thought, *Will he still remember my smile?*
My hands shook and shivered
As I tried opening the creaking window,
Thinking, *What if he never waited for me*
To open this window again?
As curious and fearful as I was,
The window opened wide.
A sudden sadness filled my heart.
He was not there.
Will he ever come?
Does he still live here, after all these years?
Will I ever be able to see his beautiful smile?
I sat there, healing my heart,
And suddenly, a paper plane struck my sight.
I looked up—and there he was,
Smiling the most beautiful smile.
I opened the paper; it read,
"I have waited for you all this while."

I pulled on my shoes and ran out to meet him.
He came close,
We held hands—*the touch of eternity.*
He whispered in my ear,
"Will society accept our love?"
I said, *"Love has no barriers.*
Love sees no gender.
Love sees no colour.
Love is love—and that's all that matters."

Like a Bird

Trusted the wrong,
Loved the wrong,
Settled for a life that felt wrong.
She dreamt of a life full of
Laughter, joy, and love.
She was offered only
Hatred, sinful words, and wounds that ached her heart.
For a home she wanted to build,
She couldn't build.
She was bleeding pain from inside,
She was wronged—she didn't deserve it at all.
She was misunderstood;
Where she was supposed to be loved,
She was ill-treated for the wrongs that weren't hers.
Her motivation was destroyed,
Her willpower was drowned,
She was caged, just like a bird in the town.
Her smiles were snatched away,
And her glory was gone,
Yet she waited still to see the end of it all.
"Enough!" is what she told herself one day.
She got back up
And faced everyone that came her way.
She broke free from the birdcage
And flew miles away.
Uncertain of what lay ahead,
She flew and flew all the way—
Her heart at ease, her smile reaching her lips.

She is free,
She is wild,
She is the bird that was always ready to fly.

Dance

Tap, tap, tapping her
Clapping her hands with small
Hits from the waist,
She rose up to dance.
Every time she heard a beat drop,
She felt music in her veins.
Whenever she felt any pain,
She danced off every ordeal that came her way—
Like it was dancing on a rainy day,
For the rainbow to appear again.
When they asked about her,
Without hesitation she uttered the words:
Dance! Dance! Dance!
From childhood till date, she chooses to dance
All her way.
Others like it or not,
She doesn't give any care.
For she knows when the tapping of her foot stops,
Her breath will follow.

Marble Seller

"Marbles, marbles, all your way,
Take them all before they go away."
Hearing this, I ran towards the window
To find a man selling these wonderful round pieces.
I stopped him
And wanted to see them all.
It was the first time I ever saw what marbles were—
Small, hard, and spherical in structure.
Every piece had a different colour;
I wanted to have them all,
But my pocket money didn't allow that luxury.
I bought a few of them
And kept them close to me.
They seemed different with the light falling into them,
And it all made me fascinated again.
The marbles became a show-off factor for me—
Whoever I met, I showed them these small,
Majestic pieces.
I kept them safe in a box
Under my pillow
And looked after them.
Years passed, and I had almost forgotten
About those marbles.
But one day, while cleaning the old boxes,
I found them again.
A gush of memories flashed
Right across my mind.
I thought to myself and laughed—
Ah! These were the marbles
I cared for a lot.

Demon

Sick and tired
Was all she felt,
Her body giving up
On her every single day.
She tried to walk the small steps
But fell back
And couldn't raise herself.
Her thoughts were eating her up
From the inside out;
The failures of her
Reminded her of all her past.
She had enemies within herself,
But to the world, she was the best.
She cried endlessly for her own,
She tried to battle all the foes of her own.
She was helped to stand up and walk,
But for her, she was unable to stand.
She was held and helped,
But her inner demons
Told her to stay.
She forced herself up and shut her mind,
For once she saw she
Could again stand for a while.
She tried to push herself to walk;
With small steps every day,
She managed to fight her walls.
She quarrelled with the demons in her head
As she started to walk again by herself.

She mummed those demons once and for all;
She lives her life again,
With all her flaws.

A Day in My Life

Coin

From the time I was born,
I saw a lot of unknown faces.
Some of them carried me in their purses,
While some handed me over
Direct from their pockets.
I have seen them all.
I have been valued by both rich and poor.
I have travelled to more places and homes
Than anyone could ever dream of.
My owners sometimes lasted for a few minutes
To a few months.
From falling on the streets
To being tossed up in the air,
My value remained the same.
I have aged now;
My shine has turned to rust.
I am still honoured by every pocket I go.
I am the coin
You are still wondering to make yours.

Cotton Candy

"Mumma, look! A cotton candy!"
Saw my daughter delighted and scream,
Impersonating my childhood.
Pink, yellow, white, blue...
Big, fluffy, sugary cotton sponge,
Spiralled on the top of a wooden stick.
"Ah! The feeling is still the same."
From a roadside charm,
Cotton candies have become
A necessity at every grand fair — and why not?
It still reminds me of the taste
From my childhood that I led.
Holding a piece of it
Makes me want to be a child again.

Chair

I was just an unpolished piece of wood,
Cut out from my roots.
Sliced and kept for months,
To rot under the rainy skies and mossy mud.
Collected by a man so wise,
He washed me from the mud of mine,
Dried me up,
And groomed me for months.
Carved on me the beautiful flowers
Of thy choice,
And turned me into this beautiful chair that I am.
I live in a godown with other chairs like me,
Waiting to find homes that
Will embrace me.
Once I go, I will make every room glow.
But my heart aches to be leaving
The one who carved me and created me, even when I was meaningless.
I wish he would keep me a bit longer,
So that I can feel at home every slumber.
I know I will leave for my new home soon,
And never meet him again,
But his carving on me will forever remain the same.

Chaa Er Bhaar (The Clay Cup)

I rise, and am given a shape
From the earth's clay,
In different sizes and forms.
I have no taste of my own,
But I smell of divine earth.
Humans pour tea into me,
And I am relished by every lip.
I hear their tea tastes even better
With my touch.
Some throw me away after their tea is done;
Some keep me and colour me up.
Some bite my edges to taste the earthen flavour.
I am an all-rounder
When it comes to being a keepsake.

Love

Gaze

Well dressed, with a face framed by a sharp-edged beard,
I saw him at first sight
As he waited for me by the seaside.
It was our very first meeting.
I saw him stealing glances at me
Every now and then;
I caught him many times doing so.
As our eyes met,
I only wished to wake to his gaze.
Until the last I breathed,
Those beautiful, deep eyes of his
Had me falling in love with him—
The eyes that spoke the truth,
So deep that an ocean could be consumed.

Reflecting

Reflecting on the childhood
That has long gone by,
It seems like a lifetime has passed.
I see a small girl, extremely hopeful,
With eyes filled with dreams.
I see a girl with a heart full of love,
That knows no discrimination or hatred for any being.
A life full of possibilities
Was what she imagined.
An entire period of innocence
Was what remained in fragments.

Holding On

The partner she dreamt of
Led her to someone lame.
Her heart was not the same.
The faces revealed themselves,
The faces she thought belonged to her.
The man she loved acted differently.
The home she was building with him felt like a cage.
Belittling was his best offering;
She kept falling for his suffering.
She died a little by little every single day,
Yet for the world, she was at her best.
The portrayal of him was that of a saint;
His acts towards her were that of rags.
She wanted to free herself long before,
But she was afraid of losing everything
That wasn't hers to hold.

Caged to Be Free

She was told,
"Grow up a little,
You will be free."
She was told,
"Study, and you will get the best."
She was told, "Be truthful,
As that is the best."
She was told to do
Always her best.
She grew up, still in
Search of her freedom.
Now she was told to go
Find herself in a different house.
She was now expected to build a home
With a bunch of strangers
That were to be made her own.
She struggled to be free all her life,
But this given freedom
Took away her life.

Escape

Escaping from her house,
She was welcomed into his house.
They started the life
They had always dreamt of.
Many promises were made to her;
She thought her talent was truly seen here, after all.
He told her,
"It's your duty to cook, clean, and manage the house."
She did so without a word,
Losing track of the days.
Years passed by,
Her dreams still waiting
To take their start.

Cape

Expected to be a super mom
To her biological child,
She ran around the streets,
Wearing her cape.
As many lives wiggled around her
To be fed,
Mother to many four-legged babies
Is where she found her real joy.
They think she saves these stray kids,
But little do they know
Who saves whom!
Her only happiness lies in seeing
Those sparkling eyes,
Wet noses and whiskers poking her
From side to side.

The Lovers Smell

I saw him sniffing from a small tin
Every evening when I used to be around.
Curiously enough, I asked him once,
"What is it that you sniff?"
Holding the small tin in his palms,
He held it close to his heart,
Smiled the calmest smile,
And said,
"The smell of your grandma."
It's been years since she has gone,
But this small tin reminds me of the times
She used it.
This smell reminds me of the times she smelled the same.
This tin is the closest I can be to her.
This small tin is all I have left of hers.

The Love Train

The train took off from the railway station.
A love story ended
Before it could begin.
As the train slowly moved, step by step,
Inch by inch,
They both kept looking at each other
Until their vision blurred between them.
As the other slipped out of sight,
One stood still on the platform,
While the other departed on the train with plight.
The cool breeze near the doorway
Dried all her tears away.
Unspoken words echoed through her head,
That her lips could not utter.
She held on to the gate,
Looking in the same direction,
But the images changed
With the muttering speed of the train.
The next station arrived quickly.
She got down at last,
And boarded the next train to the previous station.
A sign of relief covered her face.
Still waiting, shivering with excitement,
She got down at the station,
And walked her way just to find him,
Still standing in the same place.
Their tears and happiness
Knew no bounds.
Their hands reached for each other

As they whispered love
Into each other's hearts.

Chunu

As she sat near the window,
Reading her favourite book,
A small kitty jumped onto her windowsill.
She sneaked the kitty inside
And sat him down on her lap,
Reading aloud from the book to him.
It was the very first time she had ever held a cat on her lap.
There was a surreal sense of love that filled her heart,
As if she were finally sitting with the love of her life.
As days passed by, they became inseparable.
The kitty had grown into a handsome tomcat.
In his eyes, she found only love.
It was for him that she could give up anything.
Lovingly, she named him Chunu.
With her single call, wherever he was, he always rushed to her side,
Brushing and nuzzling around her legs,
Making her feel equally cherished.
He protected her while she slept
And woke her with tiny, caring paws.
A bond to be cherished
All her life long,
A bond that would speak
Only love songs.

A Love Like None

Living in this closed, buttoned space
For months now
When will I ever see some light?
Will I ever be free?
Will I ever get to see the real me?
Insecurities galloping in my mind,
Like horses racing against time.
Is my time coming close?
Am I going to live forever behind these closed, boxed doors?
Shattered by the ones I loved,
Put down by the ones I trusted
What is living a life of such misery?
Am I not worthy of love that poems are written about?
Am I not worthy of words that don't change like seasons?
I want a love that loves me.
I want a love that never denies me.
I want a love that is the supreme of all.
I want a love where two hearts beat as one.

A Memoir of Childhood

The Bell

Living a life on the bell's strike,
From wake-up calls to meal calls,
For everything there rang a bell—
The bell that reminded her of what
Time it was.
Days passed and turned to years;
The bell's ring had become
Utterly familiar to the ear.
A boarding-school life
Demanded little of her choice,
As she grew up with ringing bells
All through these years.

Leach

Living on a hilltop,
Life remained mundane from the start,
As peaceful and serene as it could get.
The smell of the rain
And the mushy green mosses
Was all that remained.
The oak trees turning green with time,
And the acorns starting to
Fall with every strong wind
That gushed by.
Walking on the wet grass seemed
A little tricky;
The small slimy creatures
Hid in the shoes in full glory.
They paced their way up to find
A bare skin
To suck out the blood little by little.
They hid in clothes
And chose to show up no more;
But when salt was near,
They felt very sore.
Walking up the hills
With a packet of salt felt ritualistic,
As these creatures were always ready
To be mystic.

Pine Cones and Acorns

Walking along the terrain
With a furry friend at my side,
Reaching towards the
Corners of the rock
To collect every pine cone
That struck my sight.
A bag full of cones and acorns
Was all the treasure I had
Every time I went strolling
Along the hillside.
Every cone seemed a little different
From the other,
As if they had their own character.
Every acorn looked a little poised,
As if they were the queens
Of every eye.
The walk down the hills
Always filled my heart with joy,
As now I am succumbed
To only concrete walls at my side.

Uncanny Corridors

Oil paintings hung on both
Sides of the walls,
Stretching a long corridor
That seemed like a sword.
One could not see the end of it
Until reaching the middle.
There was no room for sunlight to enter,
As this corridor seemed like a tunnel
That was never filtered.
Walking and running by the same
Many times,
I felt the paintings calling my name
From the sides of the walls.
There lay a painting of a girl standing with a lamp.
Every time I stood in front of it,
It gave me goosebumps like a cat.
From running around in that corridor
To writing my first letter, I did it all.
The corridor somehow saw me grow,
Into a lady from a child
Who kept her first foot and learned to walk.

Birthday Cake

Oh! The eyes sparkled with joy,
Seeing a two-tier cake
With his name.
The child who had never tasted a cake before
Cried little tears of joy
Seeing the double truffle.
As the stranger sat him down
To cut the cake,
His homeless self asked for help.
He wanted to call all of his homeless friends
To offer them a taste of this cake.
The stranger felt nothing less than a god to him
As he called them all to gather
For his birthday singing.
The kids sang aloud
As he cut his cake,
With a bright smile reaching from
His lips to eyes
That melted down as tears,
As gratitude for all these years.

Tuck Box

A splendid-looking box
Made from steel,
That looked rectangular and cylindrical in feet,
With a latch that had
A small lock tingling.
It was a box filled with many different things,
A box very close to every boarding-school kid,
As it contained all of their
Favourite things.
Whenever the hunger pangs
Struck their way,
They knew which box to pull towards them.
Every box had a different
Story to tell,
Every box had a different taste in detail.
The tuck box, now forgotten,
Remains in some corner of the house,
The box that always remained full
Is the box now
As empty as a cobbler's curse.

The Calcutta Memoir

The Wait

In the hustle and bustle of
The morning hours of Howrah Station,
I waited patiently for the train to arrive.
Tired of listening to the announcements,
My excitement knew no bounds at the time.
Eight months of long wait
To see him once again,
To feel his hands on mine
And to hug him tight.
Ah! There, the engine is visible to my eyes.
At this point, I set my saree right,
Saree, because he loves them on me.
The train arrives slowly, and
My heart gallops like a horse.
There I see him finally near the doorway,
I rushed towards him as he got down from the train.
The entire crowd outside
Seemed to slow down their pace.
All the other noises vanished away
As he stood right in front of my face.
My heart screamed with joy
As we reached each other
To hug tight.

Shobha Bazar Ghat

Ditching all the fancy places,
The group of three
Took their evening tea sips
Near the banyan tree.
A little walk through the
Old city of Calcutta
Led them three to their favourite adda.
With the Ganga flowing by
And the wind brushing their sides,
They enjoyed a few moments of silence
As they sat nearby.
Looking far towards the water,
The realisation of life felt too small.
Seeing the wrath of the whirlpools
Made them think no problem is bigger than the solution.
The ringing of temple bells from afar
Gave all the hope that their hearts required.
And seeing the sun go down,
It was time for the three of them
To return to their own towns.

Trust Me

The quiet girl, filled with innocence,
Failed to be trusted by her own mother
At an age when she did not even understand
The meaning of so many things.
Put down by her mother always,
She thought, *Where am I going wrong?*
Well-mannered, well-behaved, hardly speaking to anyone,
The girl was doing great.
But why was the mother not happy with her?
She craved validation all her childhood,
Yet received no clarity in return.
When she grew up and fell in love,
The pattern remained the same.
He questioned her for everything;
Every move of hers was watched.
His unnecessary doubts made her feel caged,
And yet again she fell prey to outrage.
She wanted to break free from this pattern
That her life had been serving her.
All she wanted was for the dearest ones
To trust her.

Registry

I woke up earlier than usual.
It was finally the day, I told myself,
The day she would officially be mine
And I would be hers forever.
As I stepped out of my bed,
I felt my feet heavier than ever.
It was as if I were stepping into
A whole new era of myself.
My chest felt heavy;
It was such a mixed feeling.
I got dressed and reached the registrar's office.
Seeing her stand in front of me
Gave me all the assurance that I needed.
She was a bit more jumpy than usual,
While I felt as if a lot of responsibilities
Had gripped me.
We said our vows and signed the papers.
Signing the documents,
I felt a major shift within myself.
I felt as if the boy I once knew was gone,
And a man had risen from within me.
She gave me her childlike look,
And I knew that
All these years of waiting
Had not gone in vain.
I knew I had to be the man
She could rely on.
I knew I had to be her superhero—
Maybe thinking it all wrong,

She could bring her own food to the table;
I knew that she was capable.
But I assured her still
To be her best friend,
Wrapped in the blanket of husband
Forever and always.